Words *for* Life

HS Press

Original title: *Jinsei e no Kotoba*
HS Press is an imprint of IRH Press Co., Ltd.
Tokyo
ISBN: 979-8-88737-089-7

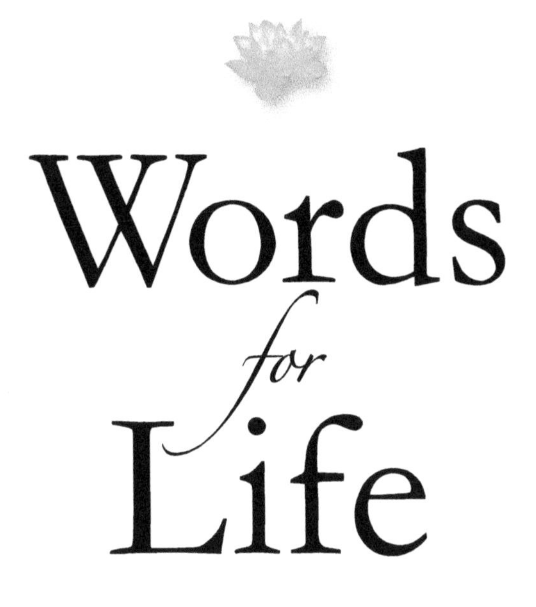

Words *for* Life

Ryuho Okawa

HS Press

Contents

Words for Life

Words for Life

①

Humans are born with nothing,

die with nothing.

2

There is nothing you can lose.

③

You are not living.

It is God who is letting you live.

The desire to protect the self is what even animals, plants, and insects have.

5

Keep your self-love

in moderation.

⑥

Treasure every step you make
every day in life.

Know that being too greedy is shameful.

(8)

The knowledge you have is
like a sword. If you don't polish it,
it will easily rust.

9

Those who think they are surrounded by idiots are by no means wise.

Always learn from everyone,

even a thing or two.

(11)

The act of easily lashing out
at others essentially comes from
a strong animalistic nature.

A man of many words is

not necessarily wise.

⑬

No matter how many times
a spoon carries soup, it will
never know its flavor.
Do not live in this way.

No love is more foolish
than one that is based
only on looks.

Down-to-earth are those
who can admit their mistakes.

16

Saying “I’m sorry” is not
a defeat but a step toward success.

When jealous of someone,

try to find their admirable aspects.

Learn from those who are older.

You are even wiser if you learn

from those who are younger.

People who have the habit of indulging in their greatest days of the past will get nowhere in life.

(20)

No one who boasts about having a high IQ in their childhood is successful in life.

(21)

Exceptional are those who can make their parents look greater than they really are.

(22)

No sons or daughters are
more foolish than those
who go around saying they are
smarter than their parents.

(23)

Some people boast about the
achievements they made
by taking advantage of their
parent's prestige.
They can only be born as sly foxes
in their next lives.

Bosses or colleagues will never approve of those who don't appreciate their parents' love.

25

People who insist on

“equality” in every situation

are failures in life.

Bragging often about your family background is a sign that you have an inferiority complex.

If you can control your anger well, you are on the Road to the Truth.

(28)

If you are dishonestly gathering money, you are on the Road of Sin.

If you have a strong victim mentality, you will be on the Road of Revenge.

30

Saying "thank you" will take you one step closer to heaven.

(31)

If you cheat your way to success
and think you outsmarted others,
you will not notice the pitfall
in front of you.

(32)

Be friends with those
who are greater than you.
People who like to be
surrounded by suck-ups
will eventually be looked
down upon.

(33)

When you become an
important figure, all the criticisms
will be targeted at you.
Just hold on to what you believe.

A tengu (a conceited person)

can realize their mistakes

only after they fall from grace.

Boasting about your educational background is just noise to everyone else.

Remember that success is heaven's blessing, and failure is your own responsibility.

If you want to be popular with women, put all your heart into your work.

Men who are always chasing after women's bottoms are no different from wild dogs.

The happiness of a woman
doesn't depend on
how popular she is with men.

Love deeply, quietly, and patiently.

A give-and-take attitude

indicates that you are mediocre.

Do you praise others with
an ulterior motive?
Always reflect on this.

Enjoying a sense of superiority by bad-mouthing others shows that you are a pitiful person.

When you are criticized
for whatever you do,
try to take a step back and
be ordinary for a while.

When you say something,

stop and think:

Am I saying this out of

a sense of justice

or out of jealousy?

Oftentimes, when you think "I don't want to be like that person," you will end up becoming just like them.

Those who have worked under others well can manage others well.

Anyone can see the faults of others, but no one can see their own faults unless others point them out to them.

A society where men want to be women and women want to be men is like a world that has gone out of order.

50

Financial success and life's success never come to those who constantly blame others or their environment.

51

People with no conviction are opportunists.

People with no conviction
defend themselves out of instinct.

People with no conviction
are always looking for a way out.

People with no conviction

are two-faced.

People with no conviction

hate to be made a fool of.

If you constantly care about
how others evaluate you,
you are self-absorbed.

A huge gap between
what people think on their
conscious and subconscious levels
makes them liars.

Women who pretend to be cute and innocent to get men are pitch-black deep in their hearts.

Your strong ego is the result of your self-centered mind.

People who tend to talk a lot do so because they don't want to be spoken ill of by others.

No one will follow those who are submissive to their boss and aggressive to their subordinates.

If you refuse to listen to others,

it shows you are full of vanity.

Everyone has

an inferiority complex.

But those who dwell too much

on it are self-centered people.

Self-centered people are pests to their organizations.

Arrogant people tend to gather a group of yes-men and form a cabinet of cronies.

If you want to make good friends,

first, be independent.

Those who think the world is full of evil people are actually the greatest evil themselves.

Earning money is hard.

Using money is three times

as hard.

If you want to be wise, read books. But bookworms who read for show cannot make much money.

Graduating from school will only give you an admission ticket. Getting the ticket to where you want to go is up to your effort.

If someone scolds you,

it means they still have

expectations of you.

72

What makes “a geek” and “a pro” different is the level of social credibility.

Don’t make excuses.

You can become

a little stronger that way.

To what extent can you accept things as your responsibility? This shows your caliber.

Do you have the habit of
reflecting on yourself?
That is the only way to
make progress every day.

Democracy is a tough system to survive in. If people stay as they are, they will fall behind others.

If you can correct yourself
with remonstrations
from your subordinates,
you are growing as a person.

Stupid sons and foolish
daughters are those who are
strict with others and generous
with themselves.

Angels-to-be are people who are strict with themselves and generous with others.

Know that you are still
a moth and not a butterfly
if you are always drawn to
a flashy man or woman.

People who cannot control their appetite will not be able to follow the rules at work either.

Being addicted to alcohol, cigarettes, drugs, and stimulants is the same as walking in the sewer wearing leather shoes.

If you live a respectable life
while staying true to your heart,
it will be an ideal life.

Do not think you can manipulate others' minds with your words alone.

Do not think of using others to make yourself look great.

Never become a person who steals others' success and energy without an ounce of shame.

All leaders,

do not be prisoners of fear.

All leaders,

know when you must sacrifice

your all and fight to the end.

Living a comfortable life
in this world should not be
your ultimate goal.
What matters most is
your true self that will live on
after you die.

Do not wish to be immortal.

Strive to be an eternal light.

Foolish people make their lives look greater than they really are, only to become more frustrated. Don't live like this.

Aspire for a beautiful life,

not a beautiful appearance.

93

Know that running and hiding from problems is a shameful way to live.

Those who are intelligent, yet cannot see the big picture will ultimately destroy their country.

No one is more untrustworthy than a loose woman.

A person with no manners

is a person with no culture.

Arrogant people look down on others. They have no love for others.

The door to the future will not open to those who are living in the glory of the past.

People without courage cannot truly be wise; they cannot make decisions or take action.

Are you sticking to your own way
out of self-satisfaction?
Or to reject the wisdom of others?
Think deeply about this.

Afterword and Commentary

It seems that young people and those who are still new to the Truth are finding it difficult to pick out the teachings that are necessary for them from the large collection of books I have published. So, I wrote out 100 essential short phrases in just one day and put them together into this book, *Words for Life*.

I hope you'd take some time to flip through this book on the train, bus, or before you go to sleep, and meditate on the phrases and reflect on yourself.

On a side note, while I wrote the phrases, I listened to the song that I wrote and composed, *Awakening*, on repeat to receive spiritual inspiration. So, this book may serve as a good commentary on the song as well.

Ryuho Okawa
Master & CEO of Happy Science Group
December 11, 2022

ABOUT THE AUTHOR

Founder and CEO of Happy Science Group.

Ryuho Okawa was born on July 7th 1956, in Tokushima, Japan. After graduating from the University of Tokyo with a law degree, he joined a Tokyo-based trading house. While working at its New York headquarters, he studied international finance at the Graduate Center of the City University of New York. In 1981, he attained Great Enlightenment and became aware that he is El Cantare with a mission to bring salvation to all humankind.

In 1986, he established Happy Science. It now has members in 168 countries across the world, with more than 700 branches and temples as well as 10,000 missionary houses around the world.

He has given over 3,500 lectures (of which more than 150 are in English) and published over 3,100 books (of which more than 600 are Spiritual Interview Series), and many are translated into 41 languages. Along with *The Laws of the Sun* and *The Laws of Hell*, many of the books have become best sellers or million sellers. To date, Happy Science has produced 27 movies. The original story and original concept were given by the Executive Producer Ryuho Okawa. He has also composed music and written lyrics of over 450 pieces.

Moreover, he is the Founder of Happy Science University and Happy Science Academy (Junior and Senior High School), Founder and President of the Happiness Realization Party, Founder and Honorary Headmaster of Happy Science Institute of Government and Management, Founder of IRH Press Co., Ltd., and the Chairperson of NEW STAR PRODUCTION Co., Ltd. and ARI Production Co., Ltd.

WHAT IS EL CANTARE?

El Cantare means "the Light of the Earth," and is the Supreme God of the Earth who has been guiding humankind since the beginning of Genesis. He is whom Jesus called Father and Muhammad called Allah, and is *Ame-no-Mioya-Gami*, Japanese Father God. Different parts of El Cantare's core consciousness have descended to Earth in the past, once as Alpha and another as Elohim. His branch spirits, such as Shakyamuni Buddha and Hermes, have descended to Earth many times and helped to flourish many civilizations. To unite various religions and to integrate various fields of study in order to build a new civilization on Earth, a part of the core consciousness has descended to Earth as Master Ryuho Okawa.

Alpha is a part of the core consciousness of El Cantare who descended to Earth around 330 million years ago. Alpha preached Earth's Truths to harmonize and unify Earth-born humans and space people who came from other planets.

Elohim is a part of El Cantare's core consciousness who descended to Earth around 150 million years ago. He gave wisdom, mainly on the differences of light and darkness, good and evil.

Ame-no-Mioya-Gami (Japanese Father God) is the Creator God and the Father God who appears in the ancient literature, *Hotsuma Tsutae*. It is believed that He descended on the foothills of Mt. Fuji about 30,000 years ago and built the Fuji dynasty, which is the root of the Japanese civilization. With justice as the central pillar, Ame-no-Mioya-Gami's teachings spread to ancient civilizations of other countries in the world.

Shakyamuni Buddha was born as a prince into the Shakya Clan in India around 2,600 years ago. When he was 29 years old, he renounced the world and sought enlightenment. He later attained Great Enlightenment and founded Buddhism.

Hermes is one of the 12 Olympian gods in Greek mythology, but the spiritual Truth is that he taught the teachings of love and progress around 4,300 years ago that became the origin of the current Western civilization. He is a hero that truly existed.

Ophealis was born in Greece around 6,500 years ago and was the leader who took an expedition to as far as Egypt. He is the God of miracles, prosperity, and arts, and is known as Osiris in the Egyptian mythology.

Rient Arl Croud was born as a king of the ancient Incan Empire around 7,000 years ago and taught about the mysteries of the mind. In the heavenly world, he is responsible for the interactions that take place between various planets.

Thoth was an almighty leader who built the golden age of the Atlantic civilization around 12,000 years ago. In the Egyptian mythology, he is known as god Thoth.

Ra Mu was a leader who built the golden age of the civilization of Mu around 17,000 years ago. As a religious leader and a politician, he ruled by uniting religion and politics.

BOOKS BY RYUHO OKAWA

Laws Series

Latest Laws Series

The Laws of Hell

"IT" follows .....

Paperback • 264 pages • $17.95
ISBN: 978-1-958655-04-7 (May 1, 2023)

Whether you believe it or not, the Spirit World and hell do exist. Currently, the Earth's population has exceeded 8 billion, and unfortunately, 1 in 2 people are falling to hell.

This book is a must-read at a time like this since more and more people are unknowingly heading to hell; the truth is, new areas of hell are being created, such as 'internet hell' and 'hell on earth.' Also, due to the widespread materialism, there is a sharp rise in the earthbound spirits wandering around Earth because they have no clue about the Spirit World.

To stop hell from spreading and to save the souls of all human beings, the Spiritual Master, Ryuho Okawa has compiled vital teachings in this book. This publication marks his 3,100th book and is the one and only comprehensive Truth about the modern hell.

El Cantare Trilogy

The Laws of the Sun

One Source, One Planet, One People

Paperback • 288 pages • $15.95
ISBN: 978-1-942125-43-3 (Oct. 15, 2018)

Imagine if you could ask God why he created this world and what spiritual laws he used to shape us—and everything around us. In *The Laws of the Sun*, Ryuho Okawa outlines these laws of the universe and provides a road map for living one's life with greater purpose and meaning.

The Golden Laws

History through the Eyes of the Eternal Buddha

E-book • 204 pages • $13.99
ISBN: 978-1-941779-82-8 (Sep. 24, 2015)

Throughout history, Great Guiding Spirits of Light have been present on Earth in both the East and the West at crucial points in human history to further our spiritual development. *The Golden Laws* reveals how Divine Plan has been unfolding on Earth, and outlines 5,000 years of the secret history of humankind.

The Nine Dimensions

Unveiling the Laws of Eternity

Paperback • 168 pages • $15.95
ISBN: 978-0-982698-56-3 (Feb. 16, 2012)

This book is a window into the mind of our loving God. When the religions and cultures of the world discover the truth of their common spiritual origin, they will be inspired to accept their differences, come together under faith in God, and build an era of harmony and peaceful progress on Earth.

Related Books

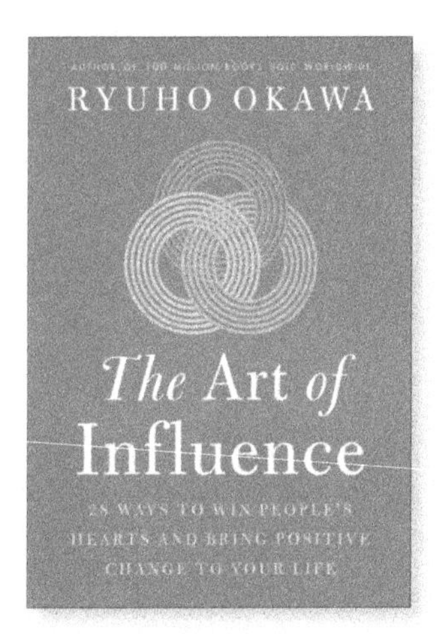

The Art of Influence

28 Ways to Win People's Hearts and
Bring Positive Change to Your Life

Paperback • 264 pages • $15.95
ISBN: 978-1-942125-48-8 (Jan. 15, 2019)

Ryuho Okawa offers 28 questions he received from people who are aspiring to achieve greater success in life. At times of trouble, setback, or stress, these pages will offer you the inspirations you need at that very moment and open a new avenue for greater success in life. The practiced wisdom that Okawa offers in this book will enrich and fill your heart with motivation, inspiration, and encouragement.

Think Big!

Be Positive and Be Brave to
Achieve Your Dreams

Hardcover • 160 pages • $12.95
ISBN: 978-1-942125-04-4 (Aug. 1, 2016)

Think Big! offers the support and encouragement to shift to new ways of thinking and mastering self-discipline. The self-proven approach fosters stability and strength in the challenges each of us faces. In addition to his relatable stories and a motivational voice to keep us going, each chapter builds on the next for concrete methodologies that, when added up, are a track to support your dreams, yourself, and your life.

The Starting Point of Happiness

An Inspiring Guide to Positive Living with
Faith, Love, and Courage

Hardcover • 224 pages • $16.95
ISBN: 978-1-942125-26-6 (Nov. 7, 2017)

This self-renewing guide empowers everyone to find strength amidst difficult circumstances and to savor the joy of giving love to others in accordance with the will of the great universe. The book will awaken us to spiritual truths that invite authentic and lasting happiness.

The Essence of Buddha

The Path to Enlightenment

Paperback • 208 pages • $14.95
ISBN: 978-1-942125-06-8 (Oct. 1, 2016)

In this book, Ryuho Okawa imparts in simple and accessible language his wisdom about the essence of Shakyamuni Buddha's philosophy of life and enlightenment-teachings that have been inspiring people all over the world for over 2,500 years. By offering a new perspective on core Buddhist thoughts that have long been cloaked in mystique, Okawa brings these teachings to life for modern people. *The Essence of Buddha* distills a way of life that anyone can practice to achieve a life of self-growth, compassionate living, and true happiness.

The Challenge of Enlightenment

Now, Here, the New Dharma Wheel Turns

Paperback • 380 pages • $17.95
ISBN: 978-1-942125-92-1 (Dec. 20, 2022)

Buddha's teachings, a reflection of his eternal wisdom, are like a bamboo pole used to change the course of your boat in the rapid stream of the great river called life. By reading this book, your mind becomes clearer, learns to savor inner peace, and it will empower you to make profound life improvements.

The Rebirth of Buddha

My Eternal Disciples, Hear My Words

Paperback • 280 pages • $17.95
ISBN: 978-1-942125-95-2 (Jul. 15, 2022)

These are the messages of Buddha who has returned to this modern age as promised to His eternal beloved disciples. They are in simple words and poetic style, yet contain profound messages. Once you start reading these passages, your soul will be replenished as the plant absorbs the water, and you will remember why you chose this era to be born into with Buddha. Listen to the voices of your Eternal Master and awaken to your calling.

The New Genre of Spiritual Mystery Novel
- The Unknown Stigma Trilogy -

The Unknown Stigma 1 <The Mystery>

Hardcover • 192 pages • $17.95
ISBN: 978-1-942125-28-0

The first spiritual mystery novel by Ryuho Okawa. It happened one early summer afternoon, in a densely wooded park in Tokyo: following a loud scream of a young woman, the alleged victim was found lying with his eyes rolled back and foaming at the mouth. But there was no sign of forced trauma, nor even a drop of blood. Then, similar murder cases continued one after another without any clues. Later, this mysterious serial murder case leads back to a young Catholic nun...

The Unknown Stigma 2 <The Resurrection>

Hardcover • 180 pages • $17.95
ISBN: 978-1-942125-31-0

A sequel to *The Unknown Stigma 1 <The Mystery>* by Ryuho Okawa. After an extraordinary spiritual experience, a young, mysterious Catholic nun is now endowed with a new, noble mission. What kind of destiny will she face? Will it be hope or despair that awaits her? The story develops into a turn of events that no one could ever have anticipated. Are you ready to embrace its shocking ending?

The Unknown Stigma 3 <The Universe>

Hardcover • 184 pages • $17.95
ISBN: 978-1-958655-00-9

In this astonishing sequel to the first two installments of *The Unknown Stigma*, the protagonist journeys through the universe and encounters a mystical world unknown to humankind. Discover what awaits her beyond this mysterious world.

Other Recommended Titles

The Ten Principles from El Cantare Volume I
Ryuho Okawa's First Lectures on His Basic Teachings

The Ten Principles from El Cantare Volume II
Ryuho Okawa's First Lectures on His Wish to Save the World

The New Resurrection
My Miraculous Story of Overcoming Illness and Death

Twiceborn
My Early Thoughts that Revealed My True Mission

The Power of Basics
Introduction to Modern Zen Life
of Calm, Spirituality and Success

The True Eightfold Path
Guideposts for Self-Innovation

The Challenge of the Mind
An Essential Guide to Buddha's Teachings:
Zen, Karma and Enlightenment

Developmental Stages of Love - The Original Theory
Philosophy of Love in My Youth

The Laws of Happiness
Love, Wisdom, Self-Reflection and Progress

For a complete list of books, visit okawabooks.com

"The True Words Spoken By Buddha"

This is one of the greatest gospels for humankind; this sutra, which is the English version of Happy Science's basic sutra, was written directly in English by Master Ryuho Okawa.

Available to Happy Science members. You may receive it at your nearest Happy Science location. See pp.134-135.

MUSIC BY RYUHO OKAWA

El Cantare Ryuho Okawa Original Songs

The Thunder

a composition for repelling the Coronavirus

We have been granted this music from our Lord. It will repel away the novel Coronavirus originated in China. Experience this magnificent powerful music.

CD

Search on YouTube

the thunder composition  for a short ad!

The Water Revolution

English and Chinese version

DVD

For the truth and happiness of the 1.4 billion people in China who have no freedom. Love, justice, and sacred rage of God are on this melody that will give you courage to fight to bring peace.

CD

Search on YouTube

the water revolution 

for a short ad!

Listen now today!

Download from
Spotify iTunes Amazon

DVD, CD available at amazon.com, and Happy Science locations worldwide

ABOUT HAPPY SCIENCE

Happy Science is a global movement that empowers individuals to find purpose and spiritual happiness and to share that happiness with their families, societies, and the world. With more than 12 million members around the world, Happy Science aims to increase awareness of spiritual truths and expand our capacity for love, compassion, and joy so that together we can create the kind of world we all wish to live in.

Activities at Happy Science are based on the Principle of Happiness (Love, Wisdom, Self-Reflection, and Progress). This principle embraces worldwide philosophies and beliefs, transcending boundaries of culture and religions.

Love teaches us to give ourselves freely without expecting anything in return; it encompasses giving, nurturing, and forgiving.

Wisdom leads us to the insights of spiritual truths, and opens us to the true meaning of life and the will of God (the universe, the highest power, Buddha).

Self-Reflection brings a mindful, nonjudgmental lens to our thoughts and actions to help us find our truest selves—the essence of our souls—and deepen our connection to the highest power. It helps us attain a clean and peaceful mind and leads us to the right life path.

Progress emphasizes the positive, dynamic aspects of our spiritual growth—actions we can take to manifest and spread happiness around the world. It's a path that not only expands our soul growth, but also furthers the collective potential of the world we live in.

PROGRAMS AND EVENTS

The doors of Happy Science are open to all. We offer a variety of programs and events, including self-exploration and self-growth programs, spiritual seminars, meditation and contemplation sessions, study groups, and book events.

Our programs are designed to:

* Deepen your understanding of your purpose and meaning in life
* Improve your relationships and increase your capacity to love unconditionally
* Attain peace of mind, decrease anxiety and stress, and feel positive
* Gain deeper insights and a broader perspective on the world
* Learn how to overcome life's challenges

... and much more.

For more information, visit happy-science.org.

CONTACT INFORMATION

Happy Science is a worldwide organization with branches and temples around the globe. For a comprehensive list, visit the worldwide directory at happy-science.org. The following are some of the many Happy Science locations:

UNITED STATES AND CANADA

New York
79 Franklin St., New York, NY 10013, USA
Phone: 1-212-343-7972
Fax: 1-212-343-7973
Email: ny@happy-science.org
Website: happyscience-usa.org

New Jersey
66 Hudson St., #2R, Hoboken, NJ 07030, USA
Phone: 1-201-313-0127
Email: nj@happy-science.org
Website: happyscience-usa.org

Chicago
2300 Barrington Rd., Suite #400,
Hoffman Estates, IL 60169, USA
Phone: 1-630-937-3077
Email: chicago@happy-science.org
Website: happyscience-usa.org

Florida
5208 8th St., Zephyrhills, FL 33542, USA
Phone: 1-813-715-0000
Fax: 1-813-715-0010
Email: florida@happy-science.org
Website: happyscience-usa.org

Atlanta
1874 Piedmont Ave., NE Suite 360-C
Atlanta, GA 30324, USA
Phone: 1-404-892-7770
Email: atlanta@happy-science.org
Website: happyscience-usa.org

San Francisco
525 Clinton St.
Redwood City, CA 94062, USA
Phone & Fax: 1-650-363-2777
Email: sf@happy-science.org
Website: happyscience-usa.org

Los Angeles
1590 E. Del Mar Blvd., Pasadena, CA
91106, USA
Phone: 1-626-395-7775
Fax: 1-626-395-7776
Email: la@happy-science.org
Website: happyscience-usa.org

Orange County
16541 Gothard St. Suite 104
Huntington Beach, CA 92647
Phone: 1-714-659-1501
Email: oc@happy-science.org
Website: happyscience-usa.org

San Diego
7841 Balboa Ave. Suite #202
San Diego, CA 92111, USA
Phone: 1-626-395-7775
Fax: 1-626-395-7776
E-mail: sandiego@happy-science.org
Website: happyscience-usa.org

Hawaii
Phone: 1-808-591-9772
Fax: 1-808-591-9776
Email: hi@happy-science.org
Website: happyscience-usa.org

Kauai
3343 Kanakolu Street, Suite 5
Lihue, HI 96766, USA
Phone: 1-808-822-7007
Fax: 1-808-822-6007
Email: kauai-hi@happy-science.org
Website: happyscience-usa.org

Toronto
845 The Queensway
Etobicoke, ON M8Z 1N6, Canada
Phone: 1-416-901-3747
Email: toronto@happy-science.org
Website: happy-science.ca

Vancouver
#201-2607 East 49th Avenue,
Vancouver, BC, V5S 1J9, Canada
Phone: 1-604-437-7735
Fax: 1-604-437-7764
Email: vancouver@happy-science.org
Website: happy-science.ca

INTERNATIONAL

Tokyo
1-6-7 Togoshi, Shinagawa,
Tokyo, 142-0041, Japan
Phone: 81-3-6384-5770
Fax: 81-3-6384-5776
Email: tokyo@happy-science.org
Website: happy-science.org

London
3 Margaret St.
London, W1W 8RE United Kingdom
Phone: 44-20-7323-9255
Fax: 44-20-7323-9344
Email: eu@happy-science.org
Website: www.happyscience-uk.org

Sydney
516 Pacific Highway, Lane Cove North,
2066 NSW, Australia
Phone: 61-2-9411-2877
Fax: 61-2-9411-2822
Email: sydney@happy-science.org

Sao Paulo
Rua. Domingos de Morais 1154,
Vila Mariana, Sao Paulo SP
CEP 04010-100, Brazil
Phone: 55-11-5088-3800
Email: sp@happy-science.org
Website: happyscience.com.br

Jundiai
Rua Congo, 447, Jd. Bonfiglioli
Jundiai-CEP, 13207-340, Brazil
Phone: 55-11-4587-5952
Email: jundiai@happy-science.org

Seoul
74, Sadang-ro 27-gil,
Dongjak-gu, Seoul, Korea
Phone: 82-2-3478-8777
Fax: 82-2-3478-9777
Email: korea@happy-science.org

Taipei
No. 89, Lane 155, Dunhua N. Road,
Songshan District, Taipei City 105, Taiwan
Phone: 886-2-2719-9377
Fax: 886-2-2719-5570
Email: taiwan@happy-science.org

Taichung
No. 146, Minzu Rd., Central Dist.,
Taichung City 400001, Taiwan (R.O.C.)
Phone: 886-4-22233777
Email: taichung@happy-science.org

Kuala Lumpur
No 22A, Block 2, Jalil Link Jalan Jalil
Jaya 2, Bukit Jalil 57000,
Kuala Lumpur, Malaysia
Phone: 60-3-8998-7877
Fax: 60-3-8998-7977
Email: malaysia@happy-science.org
Website: happyscience.org.my

Kathmandu
Kathmandu Metropolitan City,
Ward No. 15, Ring Road, Kimdol,
Sitapaila Kathmandu, Nepal
Phone: 977-1-537-2931
Email: nepal@happy-science.org

Kampala
Plot 877 Rubaga Road, Kampala
P.O. Box 34130 Kampala, UGANDA
Email: uganda@happy-science.org

ABOUT HS PRESS

HS Press is an imprint of IRH Press Co., Ltd. IRH Press Co., Ltd., based in Tokyo, was founded in 1987 as a publishing division of Happy Science. IRH Press publishes religious and spiritual books, journals, magazines and also operates broadcast and film production enterprises. For more information, visit *okawabooks.com*.

Follow us on:

- Facebook: Okawa Books
- Youtube: Okawa Books
- Pinterest: Okawa Books
- Instagram: OkawaBooks
- Twitter: Okawa Books
- Goodreads: Ryuho Okawa

NEWSLETTER

To receive book related news, promotions and events, please subscribe to our newsletter below.

eepurl.com/bsMeJj

AUDIO / VISUAL MEDIA

YOUTUBE

PODCAST

Introduction of Ryuho Okawa's titles; topics ranging from self-help, current affairs, spirituality, religion, and the universe.

CPSIA information can be obtained
at www.ICGtesting.com
Printed in the USA
BVHW011528190423
662565BV00026B/490